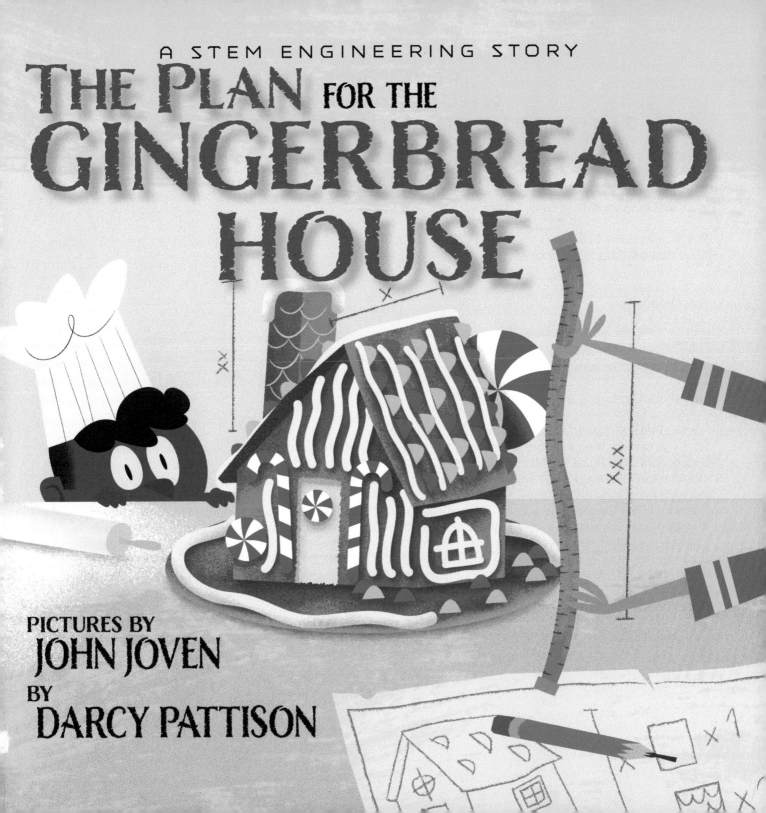

A STEM ENGINEERING STORY

THE PLAN FOR THE GINGERBREAD HOUSE

PICTURES BY
JOHN JOVEN
BY
DARCY PATTISON

FOR DWIGHT,
WHOSE AMBITIOUS
GINGERBREAD HOUSES INSPIRED ME!

The Plan for the Gingerbread House: A STEM Engineering Story
by Darcy Pattison, illustrated by John Joven

Mims House
1309 Broadway
Little Rock, AR 72202
USA

MimsHouseBooks.com

Publisher's Cataloging-in-Publication data

Names: Pattison, Darcy, author. | Joven, John, illustrator.
Title: The plan for the gingerbread house : a STEM engineering story / by Darcy Pattison ; pictures by John Joven.
Description: Little Rock, AR: Mims House, 2021.
Identifiers: LCCN 2021908697 | ISBN 9781629441573 (hardcover) | 9781629441580 (paperback) | 9781629441597 (ebook) | 9781629441603 (audio)
Subjects: LCSH Gingerbread houses--Juvenile literature. | Cooking--Juvenile literature. | Structural engineering--Experiments--Juvenile literature. | House construction--Juvenile literature. | Architecture--Juvenile literature. | Science--Experiments--Juvenile literature. | Engineering--Experiments--Juvenile literature. | Science projects--Juvenile literature. | Art and science--Juvenile literature. | JUVENILE NONFICTION / Technology / How Things Work-Are Made | JUVENILE NONFICTION / Science & Nature / Experiments & Projects | JUVENILE NONFICTION / Cooking & Food
Classification: LCC TA149 .P38 2021 | DDC 624.1--dc23

"This is the project," Miss Sheridan said.
"You'll build a sweet house made of gingerbread.

Beautiful, comfortable, cozy—
what's best?

There are only two things for the judges to test:
Will the gingerbread boy and the girl fit inside?
Will it stand on its own, and not fall on its side?

This is our plan—
Oh, the marvelous plan—
for our gingerbread house.

These are the cookies, all ready to bake.
We hurriedly measure and cut them to size.

But we cook them too long!

They're burned!

A mistake!

Still...these are the cookies
to follow our plan—
Oh, the marvelous plan—
for our gingerbread house.

This is the icing that dries hard and strong.
We whip up the egg whites and sugar till stiff—

Good grief!

It's too thin and too gooey.

All wrong!

Still...this is the icing
to glue all the cookies
to follow our plan—

Oh, the marvelous plan—

for our gingerbread house.

These are the walls that should stand straight and tall.
We spread the white icing to hold them in place.
But *this* wall's too thick,
and *that* one's too small.

This is the roof,
that we drop right on top.
But uneven walls mean
a roof that's askew.
And it's nibbled and pinched,

*and that
simply must*
stop!

The walls and the roof, the roof and the walls,
that were glued with the icing that's gooey and thin,
that were cut and then baked
to follow our plan—
Oh, the marvelous plan—
for our gingerbread house.

These are the gumdrops, each color and hue.
But someone's been snacking,
and many are

gone!

gumdrops

So, take what is left and just whack them in two
and set them in rows with some space in between.
The walls and the roof, the roof and the walls,

We glue and we glue and we glue and we glue—

It's upright again!—

The walls and the roof, the roof and the walls,
that were glued with the icing that's gooey and thin,
that were cut and then baked to follow our plan—

Oh, the marvelous plan—

for our gingerbread house.

We're done! But let's check with the rubric—
—Oh, no!
Where is the door for the boy and the girl?

So, we chisel a doorway painstakingly slow.

Be careful!
Don't crumble
or crack anything!

The walls and the roof, the roof and the walls,
that were glued with the icing that's gooey and thin,
that were cut and then baked to follow our plan—

Oh, the marvelous plan—
for our gingerbread house.

This is it!
The Gingerbread Fair is today!

The judges must study each house on display.
Some houses have slumped, as their architects groan.

But ours is well built,

and it stands on its own.
Our patterns of candies are shockingly neat.
It looks so delicious and ready to eat.

We are the kids
who stare with wide eyes
At our gingerbread house
that won the

GRAND
PRIZE!

BECAUSE...we followed our plan—
Oh, the marvelous plan—
for our gingerbread house.

This is the list of lessons we've learned.

1 Set a timer to buzz so no cookies are burned.

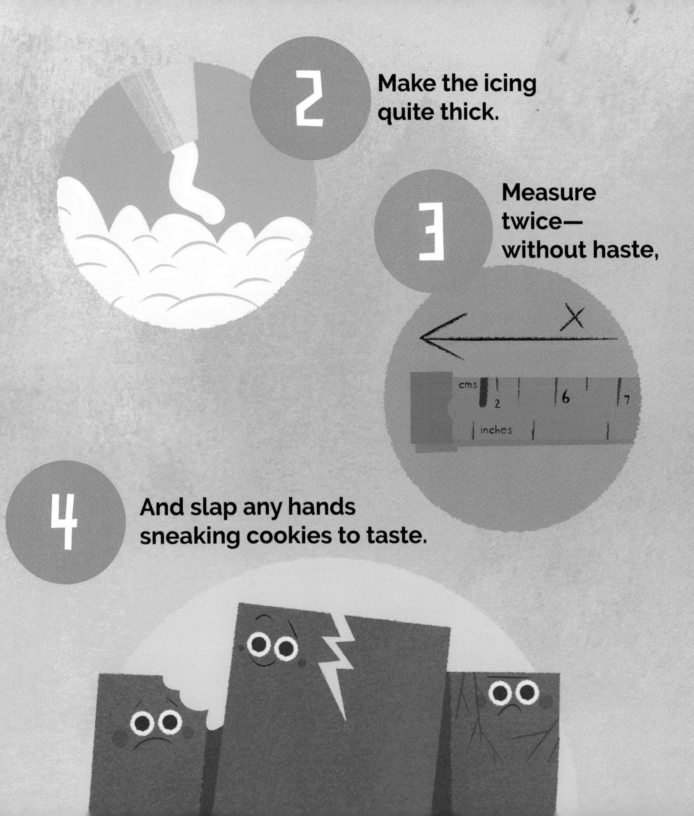

2 Make the icing quite thick.

3 Measure twice—without haste,

4 And slap any hands sneaking cookies to taste.

Let's add to the plans a gigantic front door
that opens and closes as judges explore.
And last, the whole roof needs a brand-new design,
perhaps...